Reflecting on Our Priesthood

Francis Cardinal Arinze

Reflecting on Our Priesthood

(Letter to a Young Priest)

Paulines Publications Africa

REFLECTING ON OUR PRIESTHOOD
© St. Paul Communications/Daughters of St. Paul
ISBN 9966-08-298-0
Year of publication 2008

Paulines
PAULINES PUBLICATIONS AFRICA
Daughters of St. Paul
P. O. Box 49026-00100 Nairobi GPO (Kenya)
Email-publications@pauinesafrica.org
Website: www.paulinesafrica.org.

Printed by Kolbe Press, P.O. Box 468,00217 Limuru (Kenya)
Reprinted by St. Stephen's Press Inc.
Inside All Hallows Seminary, (Near Limca.)
Onitsha, Nigeria. 08033808429.

Paulines Publications Africa is an activity of the Daughters of St. Paul, an international religious congregation, using the press, radio, TV and films to spred the gospel message and to promote the dignity of all people.

CONTENTS

V. Faith, Zeal, Truth, Joy and Love in the Priest's Apostolate

VI. The Priest's Relationship with People

VII. The Cross in the Life of the Priest

VIII. Towards the Sunset of Life

INTRODUCTION

Reason For This Letter

The priesthood is a gift. A gift deserves to be admired, to be appreciated, to be loved and to be shown to friends. The priesthood is good news both for the priest and for the people to whom he is sent to serve in the name of Christ and the Church. Good news needs to be shared with others. There should be joyful rejoicing regarding it.

To be a Catholic priest for only one day is already a great grace. Ten years of priestly life, and then twenty-five, deserve to be marked by reflection, thanksgiving, looking backwards and forwards, shared joy and prayer. As I get set, God willing, to celebrate fifty years in the sacred priesthood in 2008, I feel called to do do all these things.

As my reflections were moving in these directions, a priest friend of mine suggested to me that for this occasion it would be a welcome thing if I put down in writing my reflections on the sacred priesthood. This booklet could be regarded as my conversation with a young priest in the form of a letter. I think first of the priest in the African situation. But I do not exclude priests from other continents, since the priesthood is the same the world over, and only local situations may be different.

One can also look on this little work as one of my expressions of thanksgiving to Jesus Christ, the Eternal High Priest, for his kindness and condescension in giving me a share in the ministerial priesthood this half century. I have not measured up to the ideal which is extolled in this booklet. But my prayer is that I do not desist in efforts to live this inestimable gift each day with growing commitment.

This booklet is therefore not a research work arrived at as a result of long consultation of books and documents. The reader will not find it packed with quotations and fitted out with footnotes and a rich bibliography. The priest reader is presumed to be conversant with the basic documents on the priesthood especially the Gospels and, in our times, *Menti Nostrae* of Pope Pius XII in 1950, *Sacerdotii Nostri Primordia*, of Blessed Pope John XXIII in 1959, *Lumen Gentium*, *Optatam Totius* and *Presbyterorum Ordinis* of the Second Vatican Council, *The Ministerial Priesthood* of the 1971 Synod of Bishops, *Pastores Dabo Vobis*, 1992, of Pope John Paul II, and various documents of the Congregation for the Clergy. I might also add the personal reflection on the priesthood, *Gift and Mystery*, by Pope John Paul II in 1996.

What this work strives to do is to put some basic reflections before a newly ordained priest. It is saying: "My dear brother Priest, welcome to the sacred Priesthood. Here are my thoughts on this ministry after fifty years engagement in it. Perhaps you will find some of them useful. Safe journey".

The booklet begins with a statement of appreciation for the sacred priesthood. Four major loves of the priest are then discussed: for Jesus, for the Holy Scriptures, for the Church and for the Blessed Virgin Mary. The priest is called to follow that evangelical way of life which Jesus lived - by example and word, especially by obedience, poverty and simplicity and chastity.

The prayer life of the priest, with the Holy Eucharist at its centre, cannot be left out of consideration. This will include reflection on the Trinitarian dimension of the priest's prayer and especially on his reliance upon the Holy Spirit. All this will flower in the priest's apostolate being marked by faith, zeal, truth, love and joy. His relationships with people will bear the mark of a minister of Christ, a servant of God's holy people.

The Cross will not be lacking in the life of the priest, nor will trials of various kinds. These need to be discussed too. And since we have on earth no lasting city but seek one which is to come (cf Heb 13:14), the priest cannot fail to consider that the evening of his earthly pilgrimage will arrive. How does he prepare for this sunset of his earthly life and the opening out into life everlasting?

My dear Brother Priest, this is my Golden Jubilee Letter to you.

✠ Francis Card Arinze
Vatican City
23 November, 2007

I.
APPRECIATION FOR THE
SACRED PRIESTHOOD

It is important that the priest appreciate ever more and more the great gift he has received in sacred ordination. Let us therefore begin this letter with an effort to appreciate and thank God for this gift.

1. Old Testament Roots

Among the chosen people of Israel from which God promised that he would send a Saviour, the priesthood had a prominent place. The entire nation of Israel is described as a priestly people (cf Exod 19:6). From among this people, the tribe of Levi is set aside by God for specialized priesthood. Only they are to enter the holy places (cf II Chron 23:6; 35:5). Their role is primarily in sacred worship, but they also had a hand in prophecy and governance of the people.

2. Jesus Christ, the Eternal High Priest

In the fullness of time the Eternal Father sent his only Son to be our Saviour. The Son of God took on human nature for love of us and for our salvation. By the fact of the Incarnation itself, Jesus Christ is consecrated priest. He is "the one whom the Father has consecrated and sent into the world" (Jn 10:36). His priesthood is unique. He offers himself in sacrifice and redeems the whole world. He is priest, prophet and king. He is our one mediator between God and man. His priesthood transcends that of Aaron and Levi and was symbolized by Melchizedek, since this new and unique priesthood has a dimension of profound mystery, without traceable human origins. Christ the new High Priest, acts on behalf of men in relation to God, makes expiation for the sins of the people, wins an eternal redemption and mediates a new Covenant (cf Heb Chapters 2,5,9).

3. The Priesthood of Christ in his Church

Christ has willed to hand on this priesthood of his in his Church. At the Last Supper, the night before he suffered, he offered himself in the form of bread and wine, elements which he changed into his Body and Blood. He ordered his Apostles to do this in his memory (cf Lk 22:19; I Cor 11:25). He made them priests of the New Covenant.

St Paul is clear on the doctrine that Christ is the paschal lamb that has rescued us from our sins by this sacrifice (cf Gal 1:4), and that he Paul is a servant of the mysteries of Christ (I Cor 4:1), an ambassador of Christ (II Cor 5:20) and Christ's minister of reconciliation (II Cor 5:8). He is aware that the Eucharistic celebration is in strict relationship to the Sacrifice of the Cross: He tells the Corinthians: "As often as you eat this bread and drink the cup, you proclaim the death of the Lord until he comes" (I Cor 11:26).

Jesus Christ has therefore arranged that his priesthood will endure in his Church until the end of time. The priestly people is served by ordained or ministerial priests who act in the name, in the person of Christ. The priest consecrates bread and wine in the person of Christ. He forgives sins in the person of Christ. Through the unbroken chain of Apostolic succession in the Bishops, Christ assures this ministry of the priest in his Church. Where would the Church be without priests? There would then be no Eucharistic

Celebration, no Absolution from sins in the Sacrament of Penance, and no Anointing of the Sick. Who would then lead the people of God in the name of Christ and with the divine guarantee of the effectiveness of sacramental administration apart from Baptism and Marriage (cf *Catechism of the Catholic Church*, 1548-1553)?

4. An Indelible Mark

The priesthood is not just a function. It is much more. The Sacraments of Baptism, Confirmation and Holy Orders imprint a character. Once a priest, always a priest. Priestly ordination entails ontological change of the priest in his relationship to Christ and to all the members of the Church that Christ founded.

This sacramental character is a spiritual and indelible mark, real and ontological. It is not just a juridical empowerment, like a deputation to carry out certain functions. It is not something extrinsic. The priest is not just substituting for Christ, as a member of a meeting could substitute for the chairman who has just gone out with his cell phone to answer a call, or who is prevented from attending a meeting because of other engagements.

The priest is permanently configured to Christ in such a way that this ontological reality can no longer be removed, even in the unpleasant eventuality of the priest abandoning his sacred ministry. It is not for nothing that the priest says over bread and wine: "This is my body... This is my blood". And in the confessional he liberates the sinner with these awesome words: "I absolve you from your sins..."

The Catholic priest should reflect with gratitude that there is no other religion with such a belief of a close relationship between God and man. The concept of the priesthood in the religion and Church that Christ founded is truly exceptional.

5. Little me also chosen!

It is an awesome and breath-taking thought that Jesus Christ has, of all people in the world, also included me in his gift of the priesthood. I have not chosen him. He has chosen me. He has sent me to bear fruit, fruit that will last (cf Jn 15:16).

He has not chosen me because of my merits. If I have any merits, they are his handwork and are there, thanks to him. Like Gideon, Saul and David, I should be conscious of being the smallest in my father's house and of coming from an obscure and largely unknown family in my clan (cf Judges 6:15; I Sam 9:21; II Sam 7:18). Christ need not have chosen me. There are other people of greater virtue, intelligence, human talents and more famous ancestries, and with better cultural and religious preparatory backgrounds, whom he could have chosen. It remains a mystery why Jesus chooses this person rather than that other.

But the fact is that he has chosen me, little me, sinful me, with all my rough edges. He has chosen me to be his minister in sacramental administration and especially in offering the Eucharistic Sacrifice. He gives his blessings through me. He has given me a stole to preach in his name. I forgive sins in his name. I gather the people of God together in his name.

It is only right that I should recall the wonderful works of God, the great things that God has done for me. The priesthood is not mine. It is that of Christ. That I have been given a share in it is for me reason for wonder, thanksgiving, meditation, humility, joy, praise and determination to do all in my power not to receive God's gift in vain.

My dear brother priest, is it not important that as you begin your priestly life and ministry, thoughts such as the above should find their place in your reflection and prayer?

II.
FOUR LOVES OF THE PRIEST

6. Love Summarizes It All

The summary of the Law and the Prophets, and the heart of the new Covenant inaugurated in the Blood of Christ, is love of God and love of neighbour which it necessarily includes. This love is to be lived by each person according to his vocation and mission in the Church and in the world. Therefore, my dear young priest, it is fitting that we reflect on this with reference to the priest.

The entire life and the ministry of the priest are meant to be his own explicit way of living this love of God and neighbour. If the priest looks on his entire priesthood as a work of love and a manifestation of love, he will be assuming a very healthy and dynamic attitude that will stand him in good stead in his youth, middle years and old age, in days of sturdy health and waning age, and in times of public approval and of misunderstanding or perceptions of being forgotten.

Since not every aspect of the priestly life and ministry can be discussed here, I am arbitrarily going to select four loves which in my view should distinctly mark the priest's life and spirituality: love for Jesus, for Holy Scripture, for the Church and for the Blessed Virgin Mary. Other "loves" could also be discussed, but it seems to me crucial to focus on these four because they help to situate and orient the details of the priest's life and ministry.

There is the probability that some points to be made under these four "loves" will later appear in some form in other chapters of this letter. But this is no harm. Reality is one piece. A truth can be inspected from many angles. Let us therefore begin with the priest's first "love".

7. The Priest's Love for Jesus Christ

It sounds obvious and elementary to say that the priest should be distinguished for his love of Jesus Christ. This fundamental exigency needs stressing, because of the risk of the priest being so busy with the works of Jesus that he does not have Jesus sufficiently at the centre of his occupations and preoccupations.

It is Jesus Christ who gives meaning, unity and a sense of direction to the life and ministry of the priest. He chose the priest. He arranged to endow him with the talents and opportunities for the candidate's training in the seminary. Through the Church, Christ ordained the priest and assigned him a portion of his vineyard to cultivate.

In the apostolate, the priest is another Christ. People of faith see him as such. Because of that, they accept him and respect him. They are aware that honour given to an ambassador is given to the country that he represents. And the priest is more than an ambassador, because the priestly sacramental character configures him to Christ. Without Christ, the priest would become pretty ridiculous.

It follows that the priest should strive ever more consciously to live in Christ, for Christ and with Christ. He is aware that without Christ he can achieve nothing (cf Jn 15:5). He can fish all night and catch nothing. But with Christ's word and command, he can catch 153 big fishes (cf Jn 21:5-11).

All Christians should be Christocentric in their lives. The priest should be Christocentric more than other followers of Christ. He should be able to say with St Paul: "I live, no longer I, but Christ lives in me" (Gal 2:20). He should abide in Christ so that Christ may abide in him, since a branch cannot bear fruit unless it remains on the vine (cf Jn 15:4). "For to me", says St Paul, "life is Christ, and death is gain" (Phil 1:21).

This personal love for Jesus by the priest can manifest itself in many ways. The priest's personal union with Christ in prayer is important. Love for Christ, praise, thanksgiving, asking pardon and just silent presence before him in the tabernacle are ways of showing this loving union. The extension of the Kingdom of Christ in people's hearts should be important to the priest and should figure in his personal prayer. The Holy Eucharist, being the summit and apex of Christian worship, should see the priest at his best in matters touching the celebration of the Eucharist, or Holy Mass, and in veneration of the Sacrament of the Holy Eucharist outside Mass. The Gospels are Christ speaking to us today and will be treated in the next paragraph. The liturgical feasts which touch more directly on the love of Christ for us examples are Annunciation, Christmas, Epiphany, Easter, Ascension, Corpus Christ, the Sacred Heart and Christ the King should find special echo in the heart of the priest.

So should the devotion of the First Friday Reparation Mass and Day. The entire apostolate seen as sharing with others the love of Christ for us and winning them over to this love should be the one occupation of the priest. And respect for the Holy Name of Jesus, in a world of erosion of a sense of the sacred and of the unashamed growth of secularization and banalization, this respect for the holiest of all names should also be a distinguishing mark of the priest who loves Jesus. The love of Jesus should urge the priest on and overwhelm him (cf I Cor 5:14-15).

8. The Priest's Love for Holy Scripture

"Sacred Scripture is the word of God inasmuch as it is consigned in writing under the inspiration of the Divine Spirit" (*Dei Verbum*, 9). "God, the inspirer and author of both testaments, wisely arranged that the New Testament be hidden in the Old, and the Old be made manifest in the New" (*Dei Verbum*, 16).

The priest will love the Sacred Scriptures. They will be his daily spiritual food. The priest learns from the Church. As Vatican II testifies, "The Church has always venerated the divine Scriptures just as she venerates the Body of the Lord, since from the table of both the word of God and of the Body of Christ she unceasingly receives and offers to the faithful the bread of life, especially in the sacred liturgy" (*Dei Verbum*, 21).

In the Gospels Jesus speaks to us. The priest will surely find in the Gospels the heart, the kernel of God's revelation, the Word of God himself teaching us, correcting us, feeding us, leading us. If it is true as St Jerome says that "ignorance of the scriptures is ignorance of Christ" (St Jerome: *Comment. on Isaiah*, Prol., PL 24,17), then how much more true is it that not to be conversant with the Gospels is not to know Jesus Christ really well.

The inevitable question follows: How much time does the priest give to Scripture reading each day? Does he privilege the Gospels? Does he prayerfully engage in meditative reading rather than in speed reading? Does the Scripture gradually become part of him? If he tries to excuse himself by pleading lack of time, could one ask him how much time he gives each day to the newspaper, the television and the internet? Sometimes what they offer seems true in the morning, debatable at midday and false in the evening. Is the priest serious when he suggests that he cannot dedicate fifteen minutes to Scripture reading every day?

I know a Bishop who from his younger priestly years is so conversant with Holy Scripture that in his homilies he often quotes chapter and verse. He could give a homily which is largely a beautiful mosaic of Scripture passages. I am not suggesting the quotation of chapter and verse in homilies. Such is fine in the written text. But I am admiring what must be hailed as a lifetime love of Holy Scripture on the part of this Bishop. Sometimes I wish I had him near me when I am writing, because he would save me time spent in consulting the Concordance to get the exact quotation!

The Holy Scripture is not just a weapon to prove theological points, to condemn errors or to dress up homilies. It is much more. It is God speaking to us, nourishing us, building us up and, when necessary, rebuking and correcting us. "Indeed, the word of God is living and effective, sharper than any two-edged sword, penetrating even between soul and spirit, joints and marrow, and able to discern reflections and thoughts of the heart" (Heb 4:12).

The priest should love the Word of God. The discussions of the XII Ordinary Assembly of the Synod of Bishops to be held in October 2008, and the documents that will issue out of it, will be found of great help for the priest in his love of Holy Scripture, because the topic for that Synod will be "The Word of God in the Life and in the Mission of the Church".

9. The Priest's Love for the Church

The Church is the Mystical Body of Christ. It is Christ ever present in all those who have been incorporated into him by Baptism and who are called to live as the new family of God, in a life of faith, worship and mutual love and service. The Church comes from the Holy Eucharist and is closely related to it. The Eucharist gives life, vitality and unity to the Church.

The priest has a central place in the living out of the mystery of the Church. He is in the name of Christ called by the Church, trained by the Church, ordained or consecrated by and in the Church, and he is assigned a mission by the Church. Rightly then do people see the priest as a "churchman", although in a sense every baptized person can be called by that name.

The priest should note that in the Credo we profess our faith in the Father, the Son and the Holy Spirit. But we also state that we believe the one, holy, catholic and apostolic Church. The priest would be pretty meaningless without the Church. St Cyprian stated that he cannot have God as his father who will not have the Church as his mother (cf *De catholicae unitate Ecclesiae*: PL 4, 503A). Had not Jesus told his Apostles: "As the Father has sent me, so do I send you" (Jn 20:21)? He who hears you, hears me… (Lk 10:16). "Remain in me, as I remain in you… I am the vine, you are the branches" (Jn 15:4-5).

Of all those who should love the Church, the priest should be number one. This love of the priest for the Church has to manifest itself in concrete ways. Let us take examples.

The priest's faith in the Church should embrace the Church as she is during her earthly pilgrimage, with all her divine and human elements. We all know that the human elements can fall short. Sometimes they have fallen short, as the history of the Church from the days of Judas Iscariot sadly demonstrates. Our own personal story of defects also convey the same message. Love for the Holy Father and for the Diocesan Bishop, and loyal cooperation with them and their assistants in the ministry, are ways of showing this faith in the mystery of the Church.

Love of the Church leads the priest to celebrate

the sacred liturgy according to the indications of the Church rather than by following personal ideas or modifying established rites as a result of his own fertile imagination or creative propensity. The priest is aware of being the minister of Christ and the Church in the sacred liturgy. He loves the house of the Lord and rejoices to hear them say: Let us go to God's house (cf Ps 122:1). Pope John Paul II is very clear: "In the Church and on behalf of the Church, priests are a sacramental representation of Jesus Christ, the Head and Shepherd, authoritatively proclaiming his word, repeating his acts of forgiveness and his offer of salvation, particularly in Baptism, Penance and the Eucharist, showing his loving concern to the point of a total gift of self for the flock, which they gather into unity and lead to the Father through Christ and in the Spirit. In a word, priests exist and act in order to proclaim the Gospel to the world and to build up the Church in the name and person of Christ Head and Shepherd" (*Pastores dabo vobis*, 15).

The diocesan priest sees his incardination in the diocese, not just as an organizational and canonical or disciplinary affair, but much more as a call to share the diocesan Bishop's concern and devotion to the care of the people of God. His pastoral mission and spiritual life are shaped in great part by his awareness of his sacramental brotherhood with the other priests in the diocesan presbyterium under the leadership of the Bishop.

Priests who belong to Religious Orders or Congregations bring their specific charism and special ministries to enrich the diocesan apostolate. They rejoice to be part of the diocesan presbyterium and show it by their cooperative spirit with the Bishop and the diocesan priests.

A priest who loves the Church also relates positively with the lay faithful and men and women of consecrated life in the diocese. Of this we shall have more to say later.

Interest in the universal mission of the Church, in her call to announce Christ to millions who do not yet know him, and in the presentation of the Gospel to people of other religions and cultures, and promoting a meeting between evangelization and cultures all these are areas where the priest who loves the Church manifests his love.

Every priest can ask himself: Do I rejoice in being a priest of the one, holy, catholic and apostolic Church? Do people who have contact with me see this love obviously and noiselessly manifesting itself?

10. The Priest's Love for the Blessed Virgin Mary

A child that does not have the loving attentions of a mother is under considerable deprivation. A mother has no adequate replacement in the growth, education and life of a child. Jesus did not leave us spiritually motherless. Just before dying on the Cross he gave us a Mother, his Mother: "Woman, behold your son"…. "Behold your mother" (Jn 19:26-27).

In any case, by the fact of being the Mother of Christ the Redeemer, the Virgin Mary became the spiritual mother of all the brothers and sisters of Christ. And Christ, by taking on human nature, has in some way united himself with every human being (cf *Gaudium et Spes*, 22).

The Apostle John took Mary to his home. How he must have grown in grace and wisdom through his closeness to the Mother of the Redeemer!

The priest by being "another Christ", by being the minister who acts in the person of Christ, the minister or dispenser of the mysteries of Christ, is related to the Blessed Virgin Mary closer than other disciples of Christ. Queen of Apostles and Mother of Priests are no mere decorative or reverential titles of Mary. They are founded on revealed doctrine.

In God's plan of salvation, Divine Providence has assigned an altogether singular role to the Blessed Virgin Mary. She is the Associate of the Redeemer. She was already included in the divine promise of a Saviour after original sin. In the fullness of time, it was to her that God sent the Archangel Gabriel to announce his plan of salvation and obtain her consent as the Mother of the Son of God who would become Incarnate. From the Visitation to the Nativity, from the flight into Egypt to the hidden life of Christ in Nazareth, from the wedding feast at Cana all through the public life of Jesus, and especially on Calvary, Mary had a key role at the side of our Saviour. And at Pentecost and in the early Church she was there. Now even in the glory of heaven, as Mother of the Church, she is with the Church of her Son on earth in her liturgy, life and mission.

For all these reasons, the priest loves the Most Blessed Virgin Mary. From her he learns how to live for Christ, how to be totally self-sacrificing and loving, and how to be Eucharistically oriented. Pope John Paul II calls her "woman of the Eucharist" in *Ecclesia de Eucharistia*, 53. Mary teaches the priest how to believe without doubting, how to grow in the "pilgrimage of faith" (*Lumen Gentium*, 58), how to be totally devoted to the carrying out of the mission entrusted by Christ to the Church, and how to serve those for whom Christ died.

The priest's Marian devotion is no mere matter of sentiment, although there is nothing wrong with sentiment. This devotion is based on the strong rock foundation of divine revelation. It is not we who have made Mary great. It is the Almighty who has done great things for her (cf Lk 1:49). The priest's love for the Virgin Mary is a recognition of this fact.

This devotion can manifest itself in many ways. The Rosary is one of the most popular and best known. It should be noted that almost all of its twenty mysteries are Christocentric. Only the last two, the Assumption and the Coronation of our Blessed Lady in heaven, refer directly to Mary. All the other eighteen refer directly to her Son. And if suitable Scriptural texts are chosen to aid meditation at the beginning of each decade, it becomes clearer, how the Marian Rosary is Christocentric. As Pope John Paul II puts it, "To recite the Rosary is nothing other than to contemplate with Mary the face of Christ" (*Rosarium Virginis Mariae*, 3).

The priest's homilies on the Blessed Virgin Mary should be scripturally, theologically and liturgically well based. They should manifest the faith of the Church and nourish the faith of the disciples of

Christ. The major feasts of Our Lady are milestones both in the liturgical year and in this unfolding education. And so are those free Saturdays in the time throughout the year which the Church dedicates to that Virgin who showed great faith and love especially on Holy Saturday.

Pilgrimages to Marian sanctuaries both less well known ones in one's country and the world famous ones like Lourdes, Fatima, Czestochowa, Loreto, Guadalupe and Aparecida, are part of Catholic piety which the priest should love and treasure. Most priests in Africa will not have the opportunity to visit these shrines. But there may be less well-known sanctuaries in one's country. Moreover, every church building should have a fitting statue or picture of Our Lady. Some parishes have erected shrines to her honour. What prominent place does an image of the Madonna occupy in the priest's house? We all need tangible signs to help our devotion and prayer. When possible, a pilgrimage to the Holy Land, embracing especially Bethlehem, Nazareth, Cana, Ain Karim and Calvary, is powerful to nourish the faith and Marian devotion.

According to different countries and traditions, there are exercises of popular piety such as May and October devotions, patronal feast processions in honour of the Blessed Mother, reverence to Marian statues or pictures associated with approved apparitions or miracles, and other manifestations of love and devotion. The priest would be making a mistake if he considered himself too learned to need these practices. Rather he should promote them, provided that sound theology and the sacred liturgy are made available to the manifestations, so that the praiseworthy religious sentiments of the people of God are properly channeled.

A particular manifestation of love and trust in the Blessed Virgin Mary is shown by the priest who makes a total consecration of himself and his priestly life and ministry to Christ through the hands of the Blessed Virgin Mary. St Louis Marie Grignion de Montfort has taught a highly praised manner of this consecration as a careful meditation on his *True Devotion to the Blessed Virgin Mary* will show. Pope John Paul II practised this devotion and highly recommended it (cf *Redemptoris Mater*, 48). His episcopal and papal motto, *Totus Tuus*, is a clear and public proclamation of it. Our Blessed Mother in the Fatima apparitions asked for consecration to her Immaculate Heart and promised that at the end her Immaculate Heart will triumph.

Love for the Most Blessed Virgin Mary, followed and manifested by solid devotion to her, is thus one of the authentic loves of the priest. It is not just recommended. The priest cannot afford to go without it.

III.
THE PRIEST AND THE GOSPEL WAY OF LIFE

My dear brother priest, it is good that we bear in mind that the priest has Jesus Christ as his Master. While he cannot copy every detail of what Christ did, he is expected to follow his Divine Master as closely as possible. Jesus taught us both by example and by word. The evangelist St Luke tells Theophilus that in the Gospel he wrote he, Luke, "dealt with all that Jesus did and taught until the day he was taken up" (Acts 1:1-2).

Among the many things which Jesus "did and taught", let us take three evangelical counsels to which the priest needs to pay particular attention: obedience, poverty and chastity in his following of Christ his Master.

11. The Priest learns from Jesus the Obedient

Obedience figured prominently in the life of Jesus on earth. "Sacrifice and offering you did not desire, but a body you prepared for me; holocausts and sin offerings you took no delight in. Then I said, 'As is written of me in the scroll, behold, I come to do your will, O God'" (Heb 10:5-7; Ps 40:6-8).

At the Incarnation, St Paul tells the Philippians, Christ emptied himself, taking on the nature of a slave. He became obedient unto death, death on the Cross (Phil 2:7-9). When Mary and Joseph found him in the temple on the third day, "he went down with them and came to Nazareth, and was obedient to them" (Lk 2:51). Christ obeyed Pilate and answered him because he recognized God's authority in Pilate, although the latter was lacking in courage: "You would have no power over me if it had not been given you from above" (Jn 19:11). St Paul writes the Romans about the saving power of the obedience of Christ: "By the disobedience of the one man the many were constituted sinners, so also by the obedience of the one the many will be constituted just" (Rm 5:19).

The priest knows that the hierarchical constitution of the Church comes from her Divine Founder. The charism and ministry of the Pope and of the Bishop is of divine institution. Jesus sent his Apostles as he himself had been sent by his Father (cf Jn 20:21). "He who hears you, hears me; he who despises you, despises me" (Lk 10:16).

The obedience which the priest gives to the Holy Father, to the Bishop and to their representatives is based on faith. By such obedience the priest makes it possible for God to use him fully in the carrying out of the mission of the Church. Obedience is not meant to belittle the priest, or to treat him as a minor, or to deprive him of his proper personality growth.

The priest also shares in the exercise of authority in the Church. All those who have positions of authority in the Church are expected to strive all the time to exercise this power as a service in the name of Christ. A Bishop or a priest should in all humility and courage do what is assigned him. He does not show humility by abandoning his pastoral responsibility. That would only harm the flock. Charism is not opposed to institution. The priest is a man of communion who in the individual local communities of the faithful makes the Bishop present, so to speak, and takes upon himself, as far as he is able, the Bishop's duties and concerns (cf *Lumen Gentium*, 28).

The priest's aim should not be to bind the people to himself, but rather to bring them to Christ. If the priest were to forget that the authority which he exercises comes from Christ and is used in his name, then he might be tempted to abuse this sacred power. On the other hand, the priest should not try to introduce a type of secular democracy which does not agree with the divinely constituted hierarchical nature of the Church. It is one thing to have the virtue of humility. It is quite another to try to clericalize the laity or to laicize the clergy. The Church gains nothing, but rather loses, because of such ill-advised initiatives. More will be said on this later when we reflect on the priest's collaboration with the lay faithful in the apostolate.

Worthy of special mention in the matter of the priest's obedience is his attitude towards assignments given him by the Bishop. Of course from the Bishop's side one should expect love, due consideration for the capacities of each priest, openness to dialogue, fairness, justice and a clear vision of the mission of the Church in the diocese. If we were discussing here a letter to Bishops, we could go into greater detail on his responsibilities. But here we are examining the priest's side. The priest should allow the Bishop and his assistants a free hand in making priestly appointments. A loving and loyal attitude of cooperation and obedience is expected from the priest. If, however, the priest considers that a particular appointment or assignment given him by his Bishop will bring harm to him or to other people, then the priest has the right, and sometimes the duty, to seek a dialogue and expose what he thinks to the Bishop. Thereafter, in all simplicity, the priest should accept the Bishop's final decision. Even in the worst scenario of the Bishop assigning a duty which is beyond the capacity of the priest, or which may bring him suffering or harm, God will not fail to protect his obedient priest. God's judgement on the Bishop is a separate matter and God does not need the priest's advice on that!

We all know the principle that no one can be a judge in his own case. It is all too easy for a priest to see one side of a question, or to be sure of a certain angle of looking at a situation, without his realizing that there may well exist a larger picture on which he is not so well informed. In any case, the priest who disobeys his Bishop's clear and considered directive need not expect God's blessing. He is now on his own and he need not deceive himself that he is doing the will of God.

The priest should therefore avoid lobbying for an appointment. If he pressurizes the Bishop or his assistants through somebody who knows somebody who knows somebody, how can he be sure that he is doing the will of God? For the dissenting priest to present himself as a martyr at the hands of the Bishop or, worse still, to try to sell discontent to his fellow priests and organize a protest, is not the route for a man of faith. Murmuring is the last refuge of a coward. Challenging the Bishop by telling him that he can bring a horse to the stream but cannot make it drink, is a far cry from the example of Christ who prayed: "Father, if you are willing, take this cup away from me; still, not my will but yours be done" (Lk 22:42).

All this is not said in order to condone or justify high handedness or severity on the part of the Bishop. Unfortunately, this has sometimes actually taken place. But the point being made is that the invisible hand of God directs events, even when Superiors may be lacking in some aspect of their exercise of authority. God will always finally protect the priest who in all faith and nobility of character respects and obeys his bishop. God's intervention may seem to delay for months or even years. But it will eventually come. Some Saints have been vindicated only after their death.

12. The Priest follows Christ who lived poor

He priest is a follower of Christ who in his earthly existence lived poor. He was born in a stable and laid in a manger. The Holy Family of Nazareth was of modest means. Christ advised the person who volunteered to follow him to take note that the foxes have holes and the birds of the air nests, but the Son of Man has nowhere to lay his head (cf Mt 8:20). Christ died on the Cross and was buried in a borrowed grave.

Jesus invited his Apostles to follow him and promised that those who have left father, mother, wife, children, houses or lands for his sake would receive in reward a hundredfold, and in the life to come life everlasting (cf Mt 19:29). He sent his disciples to preach and advised them to avoid excess luggage, not to take along a spare tunic and not to be over worried about food and clothes for tomorrow (cf Mt 10:10).

It is true that religious priests, as religious, take the vow of poverty but that the diocesan priest does not. Nevertheless, it is clear from the example and teaching of Christ that every priest should cultivate the virtue of poverty. A certain detachment from earthly goods is expected of the diocesan priest. To begin with, he should be honest and transparent in his administration of Church property. In the parish or diocesan situation, he should work with the established financial bodies and loyally observe diocesan financial regulations. The virtue of poverty also covers his use of money which is personal to him. Avoiding all appearances of attachment to earthly goods and of lavish spending, he should remember the poor, the sick, the old and the needy in general. His means of transport, his house, his table and his dress should not set him at the side of the rich and powerful. To save the priest undue preoccupation with provisions for old age or sickness, the diocese should foresee such situations and arrange adequate programmes.

Celebration is in the nature of man. Anniversaries and jubilees are milestones which merit celebration. But in some countries the celebration of weddings, Baptism of children, First Communion, priestly ordinations, religious professions and relative jubilees, and also of funerals can be quite expensive. How does the priest help his people to live in a frugal way within one's means? Is excessive spending at celebrations of the rich not seen as an offence against the poor and as a temptation to young people to resort to dishonest means of making money? Would it not be expected that priests and religious become models of restrained spending on these occasions?

The relatives of a priest in some cultures can create problems for him when they expect from him huge sums of money which he does not have. They tell him that it is their tradition that the big brother should not forget his brothers and sisters. They might unwittingly be tempting him to divert Church funds to them. The priest needs to see clearly through all this, so that he does not feel obliged to support his relatives financially to a degree beyond what he is honestly able to do. And he should note that his parents have special claim to his attention more than cousins, nephews and nieces.

A test of a generous priest would be which charity causes are included in his will and how many poor people, poor seminarians and candidates to the consecrated life are going to cry at his death because they know that their father in Christ and their benefactor is dead.

The priest should not identify poverty with lack of tidiness and cleanliness in his house, nor with shabby Mass vestments and altar furnishings. In divine worship he should offer God what is best. In his house everything should manifest good taste and good order even in the midst of simplicity and frugality.

13. The Priest follows Christ who was Chaste

Christ lived a virginal life. He taught chastity to all his followers. He proposed virginity to those who are willing and capable of following this calling.

The Church has always valued celibacy on the part of the priest. Perpetual continence for the sake of the kingdom of heaven in the priestly state signifies and stimulates pastoral charity. It is a special fountain of spiritual fruitfulness on earth (cf *Presbyt. Ordinis*, 16). The Church of the Latin Rite prefers to call to the priesthood only candidates who are convinced that they have the call to celibacy for the sake of God's kingdom.

This is a witness which shines before the world as a powerful way of following Christ. Even in the midst of exaggerated preoccupation with sex and its desacralization in the world of today, a priest who lives joyfully, faithfully and positively his vow of chastity is a witness who cannot be ignored. He is the best answer to those who consider perfect continence impossible.

The priest should never forget the major reasons for this sacrifice: Christological, ecclesiological and eschatological. Through clerical celibacy the priest is more closely consecrated to Christ in his exercise of spiritual paternity. He more readily shows himself as minister of Christ who is Bridegroom of the Church. And the priest better presents himself as a vivid sign of that future world which is already present through faith and charity.

The priest should not doubt the value or possibility of celibacy because of the threat which loneliness presents. A certain amount of loneliness is involved in every state of life, including married life. The priest would be making a mistake if he tried to avoid loneliness by taking on more and more work and organizing more and more meetings, travels and visits. What he needs is silence, quiet and recollection in order to be present to God, to pay more attention to God and to meet Jesus in personal prayer before the tabernacle. Only then will he be able to see Christ in every person whom he meets in his ministry. Why is it that great Saints who dedicate much time to being alone with God are so good at meeting people? They have a clear identity. They find God. They thus find themselves and then other people, in God.

We must not undervalue the positive contribution which fraternity among priests makes for the living of the celibate life. How beautiful it is when priests live in unity and harmony (cf Ps 133:1). It is better that the Bishop arrange that his priests live in twos or threes in parishes than that they live alone. We human beings need one another in order to grow to the height of our potential. Give us communities of priests who live together, go to the chapel or Church together, pray parts of the Liturgy of the Hours together, discuss pastoral problems together, eat together and joke together give us such communities in big numbers in a diocese, and there will be better witness to Christ also with reference to clerical celibacy, as well as the general priestly ministry.

Almost in every age there are people who produce reasons to try to persuade the Latin Church to make celibacy "optional", as they call it. Each time the Church has said no, for good reasons. The latest voice of the Church on this matter is that of Pope Benedict XVI in the Post-Synodal Exhortation, *Sacramentum Caritatis*. I shall quote rather lavishly: "This choice on the part of the priest expresses in a special way the dedication which conforms him to Christ and his exclusive offering of himself for the Kingdom of God. The fact that Christ himself, the eternal priest, lived his mission even to the sacrifice of the Cross in the state of virginity constitutes the sure point of reference for understanding the meaning of the tradition of the Latin Church. It is not sufficient to understand priestly celibacy in purely functional terms. Celibacy is really a special way of conforming oneself to Christ's own way of life. This choice has first and foremost a nuptial meaning; it is a profound identification with the heart of Christ the Bridegroom who gives his life for his Bride. In continuity with the great ecclesial tradition, with the Second Vatican Council and with my predecessors in the papacy, I reaffirm the beauty and the importance of a priestly life lived in celibacy as a sign expressing total and exclusive devotion to Christ, to the Church and to the Kingdom of God, and I therefore confirm that it remains obligatory in the Latin tradition. Priestly celibacy lived with maturity, joy and dedication is an immense blessing for the Church and for the society itself" (*Sacramentum Caritatis*, 24).

IV.
THE PRAYER LIFE
OF THE PRIEST

A priest not dedicated to prayer would be a sorry sight. Let us, therefore, dear brother in the priesthood, reflect on the prayer life of the priest.

14. Following the Example Set by Jesus

The priest in his union with Jesus through a meditative reading of the Gospels, notices that prayer had a major place in the life of Jesus. The Gospels often show him in communion with his heavenly Father, especially at key moments in his ministry.

Jesus spent the whole right in prayer before choosing his twelve Apostles, the pillars on which he was building the Kingdom that he was inaugurating (cf Lk 6:12-16). After the great miracle of the multiplication of loaves and fishes, he went up to the mountain to pray (cf Jn 6:15). Before he raised Lazarus from the dead he invoked his heavenly Father (cf Jn 11:41-42). Jesus was so often rapt in prayer that one of his Apostles approached him and requested: "Lord teach us how to pray just as John taught his disciples" (Lk 11:1). He handed on to them the masterly Lord's Prayer, the Our Father.

When the Cross was near, Jesus intensified his communion with his Father. The entire 17th chapter of St John's Gospel is his sacerdotal prayer offered at the Last Supper. It is a wonderful window into the Heart of Jesus and his union with the Eternal Father in the unity of the Holy Spirit. In the Garden of Gethsemani Jesus offered his great prayer of agony, petition and total submission to his Father's will. On the Cross in great agony he prayed Psalm 22 and commended his soul to the Father.

The example of Jesus is a guide, a precept for the priest. If every Christian should pray, the priest should pray more than the other followers of our Saviour. The priest's reverence in front of God's transcendence, his awe in consideration of the tremendous ministry of the mysteries of Christ assigned him in the Church, and his recognition of his fragility and littleness, should drive him to his knees in prayer. Moreover, human incapacity to achieve anything worthwhile for our salvation except by God's gratuitous grace, is another reason for prayer. St Alphonsus de Liguori has said that he who prays will be saved, and he who does not pray will be lost.

15. Three Prayers of the Priest

We can classify the prayers of the priest under three headings: liturgical, communal and personal prayer.

Liturgical prayer is offered in the name of the Church and according to rites established by the Church. Considering that our Lord Jesus Christ is the chief person acting in every liturgical prayer, and that he associates his Church with himself in this official prayer, it is clear that liturgical prayer has value and dignity which surpass all others. The priest will do his best to be a not unworthy minister of Christ in the offering of all liturgical prayers.

Communal prayers embrace such forms as the Rosary, exercises of popular piety, prayers to the Saints, pilgrimage prayers and other organized prayers which are not liturgical. These too have their importance. And the people often look up to the priest to be their leader, guide and inspirer.

Personal prayer is irreplaceable because there comes a time when every individual should meet God in a one to one spiritual encounter. This can be in the privacy of one's room. It can be in front of the tabernacle, on under a tree, or on a hill, or at the seaside. It can be while driving a car. And it should be located at several points within the Mass, such as in preparation, before the collect, after the readings or homily, definitely after receiving Holy Communion, and in thanksgiving after the Eucharistic celebration.

Our personal prayer should be really personal. It should come from our hearts. It can be with or without words. It should not be a recitation of prayers written by spiritual masters or Saints, although such prayers can help us to get into personal prayer.

Spiritual masters highly recommend a daily prayer of the heart, sometimes called mental prayer, and, less correctly, meditation. Many such masters recommend half an hour. Without trying to be mathematically meticulous, it would not be wise for the priest to ignore this counsel. It is a bad argument for him to say that for a whole week he has not engaged in this mental prayer and nothing has happened! No. Something has happened and is happening, though perhaps unnoticed by him. As he gradually gives less and less time to Jesus, especially present in the tabernacle, the priest will gradually be getting on to the spiritual slippery slope, and the fruit of his probably frenetic pastoral activities will be getting more and more scanty. Let the priest not forget that in the Book of Numbers many people fell in battle because they went out to fight without first obtaining God's approval and blessing nor the support of God's prophet, Moses (cf Num 14:39-45; Dent 1:41-46). On the other hand, as long as Moses kept his arms raised in prayer and intercession, so long did the people of Israel continue to win in the battle field (cf Exod 17:11-12). Has not Jesus warned us: "I am the vine, you are the branches. Whoever remains in me and I in him will bear much fruit, because without me you can do nothing" (Jn 15:5)?

Although liturgical prayer is superior to all other forms of prayer, personal prayer is necessary because it helps to prepare us for participation in the liturgy, to share in it at ever greater depth and with our interior sentiments, and to live the mission entrusted to us at the close of the liturgical act.

My dear brother priest, let us now focus on two outstanding liturgical prayers, the Eucharist celebration with consequent veneration, and the Liturgy of the Hours.

16. Centrality of the Holy Eucharist

In the prayer life of the priest the Holy Eucharist, Sacrifice and Sacrament, occupies a central place. The Eucharist is "the principal and central *raison d'etre* of the sacrament of the priesthood" (John Paul II: *Eccl. de Euch.*, 31). The priest is ordained principally to offer the Eucharistic Sacrifice, the sacramental representation of the Sacrifice of the Cross. At his ordination the Bishop hands him bread and wine saying: "Receive the oblation of the holy people, to be offered to God. Understand what you do, imitate what you celebrate, and conform your life to the mystery of the Lord's Cross" (*Roman Pontifical*).

The priest needs a robust Eucharistic faith. He appreciates that Christ is the Priest and Victim and the ordained priest is his minister, his instrument. The Mass is the sacrifice of the whole Church. If celebrated with faith and devotion according to the approved books of the Church, it will manifest powerfully our Catholic faith, it will nourish this faith in the participants, encourage them to interior and external participation, and send them home on fire to live our faith and share it. This is what the 2005 Synod of Bishops on the Holy Eucharist, and the 2007 Post-

Synodal Exhortation of Pope Benedict XVI, *Sacramentum Caritatis*, call *ars celebrandi*. Far from the priest should be that mentality which sees the Eucharistic celebration as an opportunity for the priest to show off. his powers of creativity. The liturgy, and more so the Holy Eucharist, is not something that we invent, but an inestimable gift that we receive.

It follows that the priest will also manifest his Eucharistic faith by punctuality, by tidiness regarding everything connected with the Mass, by proper attention given to altar servers, church choirs and readers, and by on-going liturgical formation for himself and for the people entrusted to him.

The Sacrament of the Holy Eucharist continues after Mass. Jesus is in the tabernacle in order to be available for the Holy Communion of the sick and the disabled in their homes. He is waiting for us in this Sacrament in order to receive our visits of adoration, love and thanksgiving and our hours of adoration alone or in organized groups. The reservation of the Most Blessed Sacrament also makes possible Eucharistic Benediction, Procession and Congress. The priest whose Eucharistic faith is fervent will not be negligent in any of these areas.

17. The Liturgy of the Hours in the Life of the Priest

The Church has her prayers for the various hours of the day and night. She is ceaselessly engaged in praising God and interceding for the salvation of the whole world. She does this by celebrating the Eucharistic sacrifice but also in other ways, especially by praying the Divine Office or the Liturgy of the Hours.

"When this wonderful song of praise is worthily rendered by priests and others who are deputed for this purpose by Church ordinance, or by the faithful praying together with the priest in an approved form, then it is truly the voice of the bride addressing her bridegroom; it is the very prayer which Christ himself, together with his body, addresses to the Father" (*Sacrosanctum Concilium*, 84).

The Liturgy of the Hours is the companion prayer book of the priest. The Psalms occupy a prominent place in it. Scripture readings school us in Christ. There are also passages from Fathers of the Church and more recent Church documents and Lives of Saints.

The priest has to learn to know this book, to love it and to pray it every day. If some priests begin to omit parts of the Divine Office, or if they are no longer convinced of the seriousness of their obligation to pray it daily in the name of the Church, then something has gone very wrong. Could it be that these priests do not understand the high status of the Liturgy of the Hours? Are they less conscious of their being official ministers of the Church? Are we to believe that they have not actually made a thorough study of the Psalms, so that these can really become their prayer? Would love for the Church not be enough to convince priests to value the Divine Office? Or could it be that they do not appreciate enough the necessity for prayer in all its forms, including official prayer? If the priest pleads that he does not have enough time, could someone inform him that the Divine Office in its non-monastic form today is much shorter than what it was like before the Second Vatican Council, as older priests well know? In any case, has the priest who suggests lack of time as a reason for inadequate attention to the Divine Office, as we said before, examined his conscience on how much time he gives daily to newspapers, the television, the computer and not really essential talks and activities? Where there is a will, there is a way. There is always time for what is considered of priority.

Parish priests are also requested by the Second

Vatican Council to celebrate the chief hours, especially Vespers, with their people on Sundays and feast days (*Sacrosanctum Concilium*, 100). Many pastors are already doing so.

18. Some Prayer Intentions of the Priest

One may ask what the intentions of the priest's prayer could be. The answer is that each priest is entirely free to pray for any intentions the Holy Spirit moves him to pray for. The priest does not want, and does not need, to be regulated even in his innermost intentions. Nevertheless, it may be no harm to suggest some intentions for his consideration.

It is expected that gratitude to Jesus will figure very much in the priest's prayer. He will like to thank Jesus for having chosen him to be a priest, for all the talents he has received and for all the good that God's grace has done through him. Even for God having forgiven him his many offenses and saved him from many dangers, known and unknown, the priest will also need to give thanks.

Gratitude for what God has done for the Church and the world should also figure in the priest's prayer intentions. Graces granted to the parish assigned him, to his diocese and to his country should find in him an expression of joy, praise and thanksgiving. The progress of evangelization, including any successes in the priest's pastoral projects, should also be commemorated in the moment of prayer.

The priest should be the intercessor of his people. Their projects, their hopes, their plans for deeper evangelization and the difficulties and challenges they meet in living the Christian life should be brought before the Lord by their priest. The dangers faced by the young people, the seeking of God's will for their vocation in life be it marriage, priesthood or the consecrated life the perseverance of the married, the ordained and the consecrated in their respective vocations, and better witness to Christ in the world by the lay faithful are likewise material for the priest's prayer. The priest should also bring to God in prayer the distress of orphans and widows, the cries of oppressed women and children, the embarrassment of people in difficult marriage situations and the sufferings of HIV/AIDS patients.

Prayer for forgiveness and mercy for his people are expected of the priest. The sinners, the people who have betrayed their marriage, ordination or consecration vows, the Christians who no longer frequent the Sacrament of Penance and Sunday Mass and politicians who have not been courageous enough to confess Christ in parliament   all these should concern the priest in his prayer. He begs God for mercy and forgiveness for them. Moses in this is a model. He interceded on behalf of his sinning people when they adored the golden calf and God had threatened to wipe them out and make a new chosen people from Moses (cf Exod 32:11-14; cf also Num 14:10-19; I Sam 12:16-25).

At other times the priest's prayer is not on any one particular topic. He just goes into the presence of Jesus in the Blessed Sacrament and kneels or sits. Prayer does not always have to be in words. The fact of visiting Jesus, staying with him, looking at him and loving him, this is already very good prayer.

One thing is clear. Prayer is very central in the life and ministry of the priest. Indeed if we could with a spiritual thermometer measure his degree of prayer, his degree of love of God and of nearness to God would also become perceptible.

19. Trinitarian Prayer, under the guidance of the Holy Spirit

Christian prayer is markedly Trinitarian. We pray to the Father, through the Son, in the unity of the Holy Spirit. Liturgical prayer whether in the administration of the Sacraments, the offering or blessing of the sacramentals, or the praying of the Liturgy of the Hours has this Trinitarian route already marked out for the priest. He has only to pay ever more and more attention to the words, phrases and ideas which Holy Mother Church has carefully chosen and of which he has been made the mouthpiece.

From liturgical prayer, the priest will learn to make his personal prayer ever more Trinitarian, under the powerful but hidden guidance of the Holy Spirit. In particular, the priest will get accustomed to invoking the Holy Spirit to show him how to pray. Prayer is not, as it were, a speech which we construct on our own and read out in God's august presence. "The Spirit too comes to the aid of our weakness; for we do not know how to pray as we ought, but the Spirit himself intercedes with inexpressible groanings. And the one who searches hearts knows what is the intention of the Spirit, because he intercedes for the holy ones according to God's will" (Rm 8:26-27).

The Holy Spirit guides us in our faith and in our prayer. "No one can say, 'Jesus is Lord', except by the Holy Spirit" (I Cor 12:3), St Paul tells the Corinthians. Our recourse to the Holy Spirit to beg him to teach us how to pray and to guide our prayer, should be habitual. So should our consciousness that we absolutely need the light, guidance and strengthening of the Holy Spirit in order to share the fruits of our prayer and meditative reading of Holy Scripture with other people.

This sharing happens especially in our homilies, spiritual conferences and direction of souls in the confessional, or in general spiritual direction outside sacramental administration. It also comes into play when the priest is called upon to help a person (especially the young) to discern that person's vocation in life (marriage, priesthood or some form of the consecrated life).

The assistance of the Holy Spirit is also very much needed if the priest is to say the correct word to people who are faced with suffering, to those who find themselves in difficult marriage situations, to religious indifferentists and to professed non-believers. The priest's recourse to the Holy Spirit in prayer is also a necessity when pastoral decisions have to be made.

As a priest grows older, he should appreciate more and more the importance of prayer in his life and ministry. May the Holy Spirit grant that this may be so, my dear brother priest.

V.
FAITH, ZEAL, TRUTH, JOY AND LOVE IN THE PRIEST'S APOSTOLATE

Dear brother in the priestly calling, you will agree with me that the prayer life of the priest and his love for Jesus have to manifest themselves in the priest's apostolate or ministry. This apostolate is to be marked, among other qualities, by faith, zeal, truth, joy and love. A word on each.

20. Faith fundamental

If "without faith it is impossible to please God" (Heb 11:6), then we can assert that strong faith is absolutely necessary if a priest is to live his vocation and carry out his ministry to God's greater glory for a protracted length of time. The young priest may on his pastoral route along the years come up against ingratitude from others, scandal from his seniors, signs of tiredness from some of his colleagues and even temptations to seek what he has already sacrificed. He should remain constant in his faith, attached to his Eucharistic Lord, fervent in invocations to the Holy Spirit and constant in recourse to the Blessed Virgin Mary. He should not surrender in front of the temptation to abandon his first fervour.

The priest should learn to distinguish between spiritual dryness and lack of faith. God leads us in ways that we do not always understand. Even great saints have had the trial of lack of consolation. We are told that Blessed Mother Teresa of Calcutta had the dark night of the soul for near fifty years.

The priest needs discretion in his choice of a spiritual director. Such a director should be both holy and learned in matters spiritual, theological, ascetical and mystical. He will help his confidant to see the difference between doubt or faith crisis and a difficult passage from one form of prayer to a higher one.

No matter at what stage of spiritual consolation or lack of it a priest may be, nothing can take the place of devout preparation for Mass and thanksgiving afterwards, reverence in the celebration of the Holy Eucharist, veneration of our Eucharistic Lord outside

Mass, and filial prayer to our Blessed Mother. Under the direction of the Holy Spirit, the diligent priest will be led to come through such crisis of faith with very positive adherence to the Father, through the Son, in the unity of the Holy Spirit.

21. Zeal in the Ministry, following Christ's example

There is no doubt that Jesus was totally dedicated to his ministry. Intent on winning souls and almost omitting eating, he declared to the Apostles who were persuading him to take something: "My food is to do the will of the one who sent me and to finish his work" (Jn 4:34). Zeal for the glory of his Father consumed him (cf Jn 2:17; Ps 69:10). There was so much preaching, coming and going in Jesus' public life that sometimes Jesus and his Apostles had hardly time to eat (cf Mk 3:20). We are even told that when his relations heard of this, they came to take him away (cf Mk 3:21). Jesus sacrificed himself for his people. "I consecrate myself for them, so that they also may be consecrated in truth" (Jn 17:19), was his prayer for his chosen Apostles. Jesus saw himself as a grain of wheat which falls to the ground and dies so that it produces much fruit (cf Jn 12:24). His "hour" was always before him and he gave of himself generously right up to death, death on a cross (cf Jn 24; 12:27; 13:1).

Among the Apostles, St Paul is particularly prominent for his zeal in spreading the faith, in proclaiming Christ. For the sake of the Gospel he suffered enormously: shipwrecks, betrayals, stoning, lashing, hunger, poverty, false accusations and anxiety for the Churches he had founded (cf II Cor 11:23-28). And yet he was able to declare that he was overflowing with joy in all his afflictions (cf II Cor 7:4).

The priest also should be full of zeal to share with others "the supreme good of knowing Christ Jesus my Lord" (Phil 3:8). The priesthood is not a part-time job; it is a life-long ministry. Can the priest say with St Paul: "I am not ashamed of the Gospel. It is the power of God for the salvation of everyone who believes" (Rm 1:16), "I know him in whom I have believed" (II Tim 1:12)? Does the love of Christ urge the priest on to ever greater commitment to the proclamation of Christ (cf II Cor 5:14) so that, feeling the obligation to evangelize, he can say with St Paul: "If I preach the Gospel, this no reason for me to boast, for an obligation has been imposed on me, and woe to me if I do not preach it" (I Cor 9:16)?

Let us go into some detail. In what shape is the catechesis which the priest dispenses to his people, especially on Sunday evenings before the Rosary and the Eucharistic Benediction? Are his homilies rich with Holy Scripture, liturgy and solid theology instead of degenerating into sociological analysis, if not downright theological hypotheses? Does he nourish his people with rich television and radio programmes according to local possibilities? What steps has he taken to make the papal documents come within the reach of his people? Is he a trusted spiritual adviser to souls faced with difficult choices? Does he seek out the lost sheep and show joy when they return, without rebuking and disgracing them? How is his approach to other Christians who are not in full communion with Rome? What of the followers of other religions, religious indifferentists, secularists or self-declared atheists? Does the priest forget his duty to approach them in the name of Christ, at least to show respect, openness to dialogue and desire to share more, if they are free and willing? What of families, colleagues associations and villages which have strained relations: does the priest see it as part of his ministry to become Christ's instrument of dialogue, reconciliation, pardon and peace?

22. Missionary Zeal

Two-thirds of humanity do not yet know Christ or do not believe in him. Is the priest concerned about the missionary activity of the Church worldwide? To begin with his own country, what contribution can he make?

This interest in the universal mission of the Church manifests itself in a special way when the priest sacrifices home and culture and goes on missionary work to another diocese, country or continent. This applies not only to priests belonging to religious orders or congregations, but also to priests incardinated in a diocese. This call made to diocesan priests in 1956 by Pope Pius XII in his Encyclical Letter, *Fidei Donum*, was repeated by the Second Vatican Council: "Let priests remember then, that they must have at heart the care of all the churches. Hence priests belonging to dioceses which are rich in vocations should show themselves willing and ready, with the permission or at the urging of their own bishop, to exercise their ministry in other regions, missions, or activities which suffer from a shortage of clergy" (*Presb. Ordinis*, 10). I have seen at first hand Nigerian diocesan priests working in another African country as a result of the request of Bishops whose dioceses are in greater need for priests. These "Fidei Donum" priests need to be appreciated, thanked and supported. God will bless them for all they do so that the "word of the Lord may speed forward and be glorified" (II Thes 3:1). They have sacrificed relatively better material conditions of ministry in their own country in order to share the Good News of Christ with other peoples. In some cases, their home dioceses may need to give them material support in altar equipment, help to needy people and general financial encouragement. This dimension of love of the Church should be extolled in meetings of the priests of their home diocese. The diocesan community should also be made aware, for example at a Cathedral Mass by the Bishop, of this missionary engagement of their particular church or diocese.

May I repeat here the observation about the effectiveness of the sacred liturgy well celebrated. One of the best and basic ways for the priest to manifest his zeal is to celebrate the Eucharistic Sacrifice, and also the other Sacraments, with faith, devotion and love and with due observance of the approved rites of the Church.

23. Zeal in the Confessional

Deserving of special mention in his zeal in the ministry is the priest's administration of the Sacrament of Penance or Reconciliation. This Sacrament of the mercy of God is a great consolation for us sinners. It offers us a second conversion after Baptism. It brings peace, liberation and reconciliation to the sinner. It gives us strength to continue the battle that is the Christian life and not to surrender in front of our weaknesses and faults, even in cases that are not mortal sins. For most of the lay faithful, it is about the only opportunity they have to meet the priest in a one to one basis and receive, not only absolution, but also spiritual advice and direction.

The administration of this Sacrament is very demanding on the priest. In some places there are hundreds of people waiting at the confessional queue. The confessor needs great patience and alertness, apart from theological and pastoral wisdom, to attend to people who are so different, to say the correct word to each, not to talk more than necessary, and not to lose his calm.

The priest's faith in this Sacrament can also be gauged by seeing how regularly he himself goes to

Confession and whether he has a steady confessor. St John Mary Vianney is an example to every priest of what wonders God's grace works in people's souls in the confessional. A priest should feel guilty if any action or omission of his contributes to people's loss of the sense of their being sinners who are in need of God's mercy and forgiveness in this Sacrament. On the other hand, the people of God should not cease in prayer that God may give them zealous confessors, bless their toils and give them the joy of knowing that they are serving him so well by bringing his grace to many souls.

24. Discernment in Choice of Apostolate

A practical question which can face a priest in his desire to carry out his ministry with zeal for the Lord, is precisely the type of ministry assigned to him. Most priests are assigned parish work. But the Church also needs some priests to be formators in seminaries, teachers in secondary schools, lecturers in universities, chaplains in the armed forces or in tertiary educational institutions, chaplains to hospitals and directors of catechetics, communications or other services in the diocesan secretariat.

We all know that the final word on pastoral assignment comes from the Bishop. It is expected that he will carefully consult both the needs of the diocese and the talents and general disposition of the priest to be appointed. Here come into consideration the leadership style of the Bishop, the quality of his advisers and the flexibility of the priest who is to be given an assignment. This priest will cooperate best when he brings his gifts of nature and grace, of intelligence and will, to carry out an assignment. There can arise difficult situations in which it is not easy to assign fault. I have found it personally enriching for me and spiritually the safest, not to lobby my superiors for any assignment, but to try to see the invisible hand of God in their decisions. In an earlier chapter I have already said that the priest has the right, and even the duty, to expose his mind on a possible assignment, if he considers it clearly above his powers, or if he foresees harm to himself or to others. When all that is done, he should entrust himself to the caring hands of divine Providence.

Similar to the question of assignment is the matter of whether a priest should be assigned to do any further specialized studies after ordination, and if so, what. Comments to be made are more or less similar to what I have just proposed on pastoral assignment. Of course the Church and the society need some priests who have done specialized courses. A problem can arise when a priest begins to function as a judge in his own case and to consider that he has the right to be assigned to a particular study course. There is also a problem when the Bishop or his advisers do not sufficiently weigh the needs of Church and society or the talents of individual priests. Openness is needed on the side of both the priest and the Bishop. If the priest does not accept the final decision of the Bishop, how can such a priest argue that he is doing the will of God rather than following his own personal preference? In God's will is our peace.

25. Preaching the Cross of Christ

The ministry of the priest calls on him to preach the Gospel without discount. Not everything that Jesus asks us to do in following him is easy or pleasant. He also invites all those who want to be his disciples to take up their cross daily and follow him (cf Lk 9:23). He made demands which only God can make: "Whoever loves father or mother more than me is not worthy of me, and whoever loves son or daughter more than me is not worthy of me; and whoever does not take up his cross and follow after me is not worthy of me. Whoever finds his life will lose it, and whoever loses his life for my sake will find it" (Mt 10:37-39).

Christ's commandments to love one another, to forgive those who do us evil, to be honest and chaste, sometimes go against the current of public opinion. People find these precepts hard going.

Here are examples that come to mind. How do we convince a person to forgive the one who accused him falsely and so ruined his promotion prospects or his entire job, or to forgive the person who killed his brother? In money matters, how is an official to be persuaded not to take bribes when his colleagues are doing just that? Some people sell fake drugs or expired ones or cheat in other ways in the market and grow rich. They tell the Christian who wants to be fully honest that he will not get rich in that way. There are students who are threatened with failure or low marks in examinations if they do not go along with the morally unacceptable suggestions of their teachers.

There are also Catholics who find themselves in situations that disqualify them from reception of Penance and Holy Communion as long as those situations persist. Examples are divorced and remarried. And there are innocent husbands or wives who have been abandoned by their partner and who nevertheless are not free to find new consorts. There are couples who may have good reasons for wanting to postpone the arrival of the next child, but who are being persuaded by people to adopt means which the Church has clearly declared to be against the law of God.

It is not easy to preach the full Gospel to people in these and similar situations. On the one hand, the priest is to show compassion, love and kindness. On the other hand, he is only a servant of Jesus Christ and has no power to modify the demands of God's law of right and wrong. He can only explain them according to the handed-down teaching of the Church and the advice given by sound theologians in the more difficult cases.

What the priest should totally avoid is the setting up of what is regarded by some as a pastoral approach against what is clear as the stand of the Catholic faith. The rules of right and wrong are not subject to the market forces of opinion poll or popular practice. St Paul was very clear in his instructions to his disciple Timothy: "I charge you in the presence of God and of Christ Jesus, who will judge the living and the dead, and by his appearing and his kingly power: proclaim the word; be persistent whether it is convenient or inconvenient; convince, reprimand, encourage through all patience and teaching. For the time will come when people will not tolerate sound doctrine but, following their own desires and insatiable curiosity, will accumulate teachers and will stop listening to the truth and will be delivered to myths" (II Tim 4:1-4).

The priest should be clear on the point that he has no authority to make a discount on the ten commandments of God. Only the truth will make people free (cf Jn 8:32). Orthopraxis is not only not opposed to orthodoxy but genuine pastoral practice follows from true doctrine. Clerics who pretend that they can modify the demands of God's law should not parade themselves as "pastorally minded", or as compassionate. They should preach the word of God with all courage and kindness, and allow divine grace to work in peoples' hearts with the cooperation which grace can enable.

26. Joy in the Priest's Ministry

The ministry of the priest should be marked by joy. The Gospel is the Good News of salvation in Jesus

Christ. The priest is happy to have been given the treasure of the faith, to have been invited to the banquet of the Lamb of God, initially in this world in the Church, and permanently in heaven. This is reason for joy, not sadness. A feast has the distinguishing mark of joy.

When the priest celebrates Mass, ministers the other Sacraments, preaches to the people and catechizes them, his joy at sharing the riches of Christ should come across as genuine. And the people will catch it. Joy shared is joy multiplied. The priest does not want to monopolize the riches of the mysteries of Christ. He wants to share them.

When people approach a priest for advice, when he visits them, when they sit with him for hours at a parish or other meeting, they should come away convinced that this man is happy in his vocation, that he believes himself to have a precious treasure and that he really wants to share these riches with other people.

When people listen to the priest in church, they are not looking for a show of learning or for theological gymnastics. They want to receive the pure and living spring of the word of God delivered without diluting elements. They want to see the priest's conviction and joy. The word of God has power to work in people's hearts (cf Heb 5:12).

We all know that saying of Pope Paul VI that the world listens to witnesses rather than teachers, and that if it listens to teachers, it is because they are first witnesses. The priest who lives his priestly life in quiet joy and announces the Gospel with his life and thus with conviction and joy, is an irrefutable witness.

27. Love for the People in the Priest's Ministry

The priest who carries out his ministry with zeal, fidelity to the Gospel and joy, will also be one who loves the people entrusted to him. One of the ways in which he shows this love for them is to be near them in all stages of life.

He baptizes them, thus incorporating them in Christ and the Church. If the person to be baptized is a baby, the priest takes the occasion to catechize the parents. Some parents do not frequent the sacraments or are in irregular marriage situations. This is a golden opportunity for the priest to meet them.

The priest shows priestly love for young people by introducing them into the faith through adequate catechesis, by preparing them for the Sacraments of Penance, Confirmation and the Holy Eucharist and by helping them discern their vocation to the priesthood, the consecrated life or the married state.

In view of the crucial importance of marriage and the family for both Church and society, the priest helps intending marriage partners to prepare themselves by the virtues of honesty, hard work, chastity and flexibility. Near to the wedding day, he arranges suitable courses to prepare them for marriage. He does all in his power to make the wedding celebration a thing of joy for the spouses and their friends. He follows up married couples especially by making use of the several marriage enrichment programmes and associations in the Church. He does not abandon people in improper marriage situations. And he seeks adequate help for widows and orphans.

Candidates for the priesthood and for the consecrated life need to find in the priest a loving father. They will always need advice and the ministration of the Sacraments of Penance and the Holy Eucharist. Some of them come from poor families and may need financial help. Where the priest is not able to provide funds for them all by himself, he should at least be able to find and motivate benefactors.

Many candidates for the priesthood in the countries of recent evangelization have been trained for years in seminaries because of the generosity of men and women benefactors in older Churches in Europe and North America. And these benefactors, following the example of the French lady, Jeanne Bigard, who began what was later elevated to the status of the Pontifical Society of St Peter the Apostle for Mission Clergy, are generally not rich people. But they are generous. It would be expected of priests from these countries recently evangelized, that they would become promoters of help for financially poor candidates to the priesthood or the consecrated life.

The priest shows love for his people by being near them in moments of sorrow and suffering: sickness, accidents, hospitalization, old age and death. The priest, when he conducts Requiem Masses and burials, should carry out the sacred rites in a way that manifests his sharing of the grief of the bereaved, and not as an unfeeling philosopher or a detached functionary. His homily should also allow his sorrow to come across. It may happen that some Catholic communities in some African countries are rather demanding on the relatives of the dead because of some Church or association fees which the deceased should have paid. The wise and loving priest will know how to temper such demands with Gospel compassion and mercy, especially at the time when the family of the bereaved is just asking for Church burial for their dear one.

It is also part of love to share other people's joy: marriage, priestly ordination, religious profession, Baptism of a child, blessing of a new house, jubilees and promotion in one's job. The priest should remember the principle already stated, that joy shared is joy multiplied. To refuse or forget to share the joy of another can be interpreted to mean that one does not care much for that person.

One of the ways in which the priest shows his love for his people is in giving them blessing. It is a sad commentary on a people's faith when they no longer ask for the priest's blessing or no longer welcome it with joy.

The priest should be convinced that one of his assignments at ordination is to call down God's blessing on people and on things and places. It is no act of humility on his part if he shies away from this ministry. He should note that it is not really his blessing. He is just God's instrument. The usual formula is: "May the blessing of Almighty God, the Father, and the Son and the Holy Spirit, descend upon you and remain with you always", or "May Almighty God bless you, the Father, and the Son and the Holy Spirit".

The priest should not forget that his hands have been consecrated and his palms anointed. Why is he so sparing in imposing hands on people's heads or shoulders? We are body and soul. The Church has always valued symbols and gestures, such as the imposition of hands. This can mean a blessing, or a sending on mission or a conferring of an Order or Sacrament. Too much intellectualistic abstraction in this matter is mistaken. It is quite in order for the priest to impose hands on people when he blesses them.

When the priest blesses people outside a strictly liturgical setting and in less formal circumstances, there is no reason why before the actual blessing formula he should not construct a rich prayer to call down God's blessing on this son/daughter of his for good health, safety in a forthcoming journey, success in examinations, protection from evil spiritual and temporal, discernment in difficult situations, wisdom in meetings about to be held, fruitfulness in marriage, recovery of lost articles, and solution to situations of misunderstanding or tension in families, parishes, dioceses or religious congregations. Indeed such prayers, if well constructed, can instruct, comfort and encourage people during difficult situations in their earthly pilgrimage.

It goes without saying that in liturgical blessings, the priest should keep to approved texts. But even such texts often provide for a Prayer of the Faithful or Bidding Prayers where the needs of the community or persons in question can be more precisely articulated.

The priest's love for his people should be a distinguishing mark of his ministry. Occasions will not be lacking to manifest this love of the pastor. Every priest can ask himself how he stands when examined on these matters.

VI.
THE PRIEST'S
RELATIONSHIP WITH PEOPLE

The priest is ordained for the people. He necessarily has to have relationships with people. It is important both for the priest and for the people that the priest develops a healthy and Gospel-inspired attitude on this matter from the very beginning of his priestly ministry. So, dear brother, let us make the following reflections. The preceding chapter has considered these relationships from the point of view of zeal in the apostolate and its allied qualities of truth, joy and love. There are other aspects which merit separate attention, such as respect and availability. We should also focus on the three categories of persons in the Church with whom the priest relates: priests, lay faithful and consecrated men and women.

28. The Priest's Respect for every human being

Every human being merits respect. It is most edifying to notice in the Gospel how our beloved Lord and Saviour Jesus Christ showed respect for everyone, be they the Apostles or the people who challenged his authority, the Bethany friends, Martha, Mary and Lazarus, or the pharisees and scribes who attributed his miracles to Beelzebul. Jesus respected Zacchaeus, the woman surprised in adultery and the centurion who requested a miracle. He welcomed the heavy crowds who came to hear the word of God; he healed those who were sick; and he fed the hungry. He handled in an admirable way the soldiers who were sent to arrest him, the curious Herod, the cowardly Pilate and even those who mocked him when he was in agony on the Cross.

The priest learns from Jesus to respect people. He looks on the face of every human being and in faith sees Christ. He remembers the words of his Master that what he does for the least of these little ones, he does for Christ.

The priest who respects people shows this in many ways. He welcomes those who seek his attention or who visit him. He might be tired after long hours in the confessional or visiting the parish. But he does not forget that sometimes the people who most need his pastoral attention do not come at the ideal time for him. He listens to people. This sounds simple. And yet it is fundamental. A good doctor knows that it is not enough for him to know the diagnosis. It is also part of healing for him to listen to the patient and not to rush him and become impatient.

The respectful priest gives credit where credit is due. When people sit with him at meetings they realize that he is ready, not only to give but also to receive. He does not hesitate to change his position in the light of better and more complete information. The stubborn person who refuses to listen or to change, and who adopts the unwritten principle: "Don't confuse me with facts", is not respectful of other people.

One of the ways in which the priest shows respect for people is to answer their letters (and today often emails) promptly. Every extra day of delay means just a little less respect for the other person. No one enjoys receiving a reply after several months with the excuse that the priest was rather busy. This excuse implies that there were other matters more deserving of attention than this letter. No one is amused to be treated that way. On the other hand, everyone is flattered to get an immediate response. I do not want to exaggerate. There are letters which raise difficult issues that demand days, or even weeks, of research before an adequate answer can be found. And there may be letters which contain hidden traps or dangers, and which demand great prudence on the part of the priest who replies, because written things remain. But most letters which the priest receives are not of this category. They can be answered rather quickly, and in a few lines. The priest who is allergic to answering letters may need someone to inform him that one of the surest ways to lose friends is to ignore their letters (or emails), because they draw the conclusion that they are being told that they do not count for much.

29. The Priest's Availability

Availability follows on respect and love for people. Various people call on the priest, and not always at the most convenient times for him. He should be afraid of having that load on his conscience caused by people calling, not being received by him, turning away disappointed, and never returning.

There are those who need the priest to hear their confessions, to listen to their spiritual problems or simply to examine their suggestions on how the parish apostolate could be improved upon.

There are callers who are looking for money, food, clothing or other material necessities. It is not always easy to distinguish between the really needy and the expert professional seekers who know how to go from one rectory to another to present disaster stories. It is a lesser evil that the priest be deceived by one such person, than that he turn away a really suffering member of Christ.

There are also people who are waiting for the priest to visit them: the old, the sick at home or in hospital, the families in difficulty, the people who are celebrating a joyful event, and people who have lost their dear ones. Has the priest set up with the parish council a small committee that serves as the eyes, the ears, the hands and the feet of the parish community in finding out and going to help the needy, the lonely, the old and the sick? A parish should be a community, not only of faith and worship, but also of charity. Pope Benedict XVI says that a Eucharistic celebration which does not lead to works of charity or solidarity is fragmented (cf. *Deus Caritas Est*, 14).

Do people who meet the priest come away with the conviction: I have met a man of God. I have seen God in a man?

The priest has to be available to his Bishop, his brother priests, to the lay faithful and to consecrated men and women. Let us take these relationships one after the other.

30. The Priest's Relationship with his Bishop

It matters very much for the internal peace and joy of the priest and for his life of union with God, what type of relationship he has with his Bishop. We all know that faith is a basic necessity in this relationship. The priest should see the Bishop as his father in Christ, the chief liturgist in the diocese, the coordinator of the diocesan apostolate, and the leader of the diocesan presbyterium or priestly brotherhood.

Such faith will lead the priest to accept and respect his Bishop, to cooperate sincerely with him and to desire that the diocesan apostolate may succeed. Loyalty to the Bishop includes both obedience to him and also honesty in telling him truthfully how one sees a situation, even if, and especially when, the Bishop sees it differently. A loyal priest does not hide his views from the Bishop. He does not give advice according to what he calculates that he will gain. He is ready to risk popularity with the Bishop when it comes to expressing his views. He is not an ecclesiastical politician. His one concern is that the Kingdom of God may flourish. All this is easier to say than to do. But the courageous priest should not find it impossible, with the grace of God. And the Bishop should regard those priests who tell him the situation as they honestly see it, as his very precious advisers, friends and co-workers.

It follows that between the Bishop and his priests, the charity of Christ should be the rule and guide, the climate and the style, under the guidance of the Holy Spirit. The priest is not a soldier who just carries out orders. And the Bishop is not a commanding officer. They are both workers in the vineyard of Christ.

The priest should not set too much value on whether the Bishop was once his classmate, or whether they originate from the same parish, or whether they have other friendship ties that make them develop a liking for each other. The relationship between them is better built on supernatural faith and charity and on love of Christ and the Church. Such solid foundations will stand the priest in good stead when the Bishop he likes is transferred or dies and another Bishop arrives with whom he has no long-standing friendship. This faith of the priest can also be tested when a diocese is divided. At such a juncture, a priest can be tempted to choose to go to the diocese where his Bishop "friend" goes. Strong faith will help the priest to make a decision based on better foundations.

As every human being has defects, so has every Bishop. A priest will beg the Lord to give him the grace to work with his real and present Bishop, and not wait for an imaginary one. The invisible hands of Divine Providence, as already discussed above, will always protect the loyal and faith-filled priest.

31. The Priest's Association with his Brother Priests

The priest knows that he has not been ordained to carry out the ministry all on his own, but rather with his brother priests, under the leadership of his Bishop. With his brother priests in the diocese he forms a presbyterium, a sacramental brotherhood (cf. *Presbyt. Ordinis*, 7).

It is not only edifying for the lay faithful and the religious to see their priests living together, working together, praying together, eating together and playing together. It is also a great sustaining help for the priest to be part of this sacerdotal community. The younger priests learn from the more experienced and the older priests do not disdain picking up a few fresh elements and pastoral approaches from the young.

If Jesus has promised to be in the midst of those who gather in twos or threes in his name (cf. Mt 18:20), how much more will a community of priests who gather for their prayers together or for pastoral discussion find Jesus in their midst! This consideration helps us to appreciate the beauty, and even importance, of priests in a diocese gathering together for their monthly recollection or for their annual retreat, preferably with their Bishop. The diocesan Bishop occasionally calls a meeting of his priests for pastoral discussion, or gets such organized in deaneries. A priest who does not participate in such important acts of his presbyterium would be making a mistake.

It is expected that a priest will share the joys and sorrows of his brother priests. Occasions of joy that spring to mind are ordination anniversaries and jubilees. But there are also parish celebrations where the presence of other priests increases the joy of the parish priest and his parishioners. Attendance at funerals of other priests is regarded as a priority in most places. Since the family spirit is rather strong in African countries, priests also participate at the funerals of close relatives of their priest colleagues. The high number of priests on such occasions is an eloquent testimony to their sacramental brotherhood. It is louder than a homily on mutual love.

Sometimes a priest can be misunderstood, or seem to be forgotten by the central diocesan administrators. His relationship with some other priest or with his Bishop can get tensed up for one reason or the other. There can be difficulties in matters touching financial administration. An innocent priest can be suspected of not being transparent in how he looks after parish money. In all such cases, priests who can be help to remedy the situation should come near their colleague to help as best they can.

It is not unheard of that there can arise cases of accusation or suspicion of immoral conduct against a priest. The priest may be innocent; or he may not be; or it may be impossible to know the facts. Whatever the case may be, his brother priests are not expected to abandon the priest. It is true that prudence will be needed so as not to make the situation worse by appearing to sit in judgment and acquitting or condemning. The Fathers of the Second Vatican Council urge a fraternal spirit among priests: "They will be particularly solicitous for priests who are sick, afflicted, overburdened with work, lonely, exiled from their homeland, or suffering persecution" (*Presbyt. Ordinis*, 8). We might also add: accused, suspended, suspected or compulsorily retired. The charity and spiritual wisdom of each priest will indicate to him how to be a brother to such priests in difficulty.

32. Avoiding Bad Company between Priests

While community life in some from is to be encouraged between priests, it is also not impossible that from time to time there may be one or two priests who give bad example to their fellow priests. Perhaps they are discontented with the Bishop or the diocesan administration. May be they are angry with the Pope and Rome. It can happen they ignore prayer and court dangerous company. There may be problems of lack of transparent financial administration. And such priests can be unhappy clerics who try to sell their discontent to their fellow priests.

Even though the picture which I have just painted may be considered exaggerated, human nature being fragile as we know it, it should not cause total surprise if one or more of these phenomena become reality.

The younger priest is generally more vulnerable in such situations than his older colleagues. He will, on the one hand, avoid making rash judgements on his colleagues or formulating declarations on situations which he may not entirely understand. On the other hand, he needs much courage, spiritual wisdom and discernment to navigate his way out of the company of such priests. If it is possible for him to contribute with brotherly correction, even in the softest of ways, he should try to do so. Sometimes the best counsel is for him to avoid such company. He will profit from the advice of a good and wise spiritual director. The young priest should never consent to buy discontent from anyone. Rather he should everyday reconsecrate himself to the God of his joy, God who gives joy to his youth (cf. Ps 43:4).

33. The Priest's Relationship with the Lay Faithful

The lay faithful constitute more than 98% of the Church. The priest's relationship with the lay faithful has to be built on good ecclesiology, on clarity about the identity of the lay faithful and the identity of the priest. The lay faithful are those Christians who are incorporated into Christ and the Church by Baptism and who, unlike priests and religious, are called to live their share in the priestly, prophetic and kingly office of

Christ in the secular sphere. By the secular sphere is meant the earthly realities in which the lay faithful live and work: the family, work and recreation, science and technology, the arts and professions, politics and government and the mass media. "The laity must take on the renewal of the temporal order as their own special obligation" (*Apost. Actuositatem*, 7). "For the lay faithful to be present and active in the world is not only an anthropological and sociological reality, but in a specific way, a theological and ecclesiastical reality as well (John Paul II: *Christifideles Laici*, 15).

The priest should therefore encourage the lay faithful to carry out their own apostolate. He cannot replace them in that. From him, they will receive doctrine and sacramental administration. Then in the secular arena "let the layman take on his own distinctive role" (*Gaudium et Spes*, 43). The priest should allow the lay faithful in their apostolate to have "that just freedom which belongs to everyone in this earthly city" (*Lumen Gentium*, 37).

The priest has nothing to fear from the laity who are conscious of their specific role and who are employed in carrying it out. Genuine lay apostolate is no threat to the priestly vocation. The two apostolates complement each other. Collaboration and mutual respect between clerics and laity reinforces both vocations and is in line with good ecclesiology.

When the lay faithful strive to animate or christianize the temporal order, they are not doing a favour to the priest. The whole mission of the Church is not meant to be carried out by the priests alone. The lay faithful have their irreplaceable role to fulfil.

On the other hand, harm can be done to the Church by the confusion of roles or identities. Attempts to clericalize the laity should not be regarded as promotion of the laity.

It is, for example, wrong for priests to sit down at Mass and ask the laity, the extraordinary ministers of Holy Communion, to distribute Holy Communion. It is likewise no promotion for a pastoral assistant to be asked to deliver the homily at Mass. This is the role of the priest or the deacon.

The priest who has the correct approach to collaboration with the lay faithful knows how to assign them roles in the catechetical instruction of various categories of people and how to encourage them to exercise leadership roles in youth groups, Catholic associations and movements. He sets up programmes to educate them in political engagement and participation and in the difficult but necessary leadership needed within professional bodies like the bar association or the doctors guild, so that witness can be effectively given to Christ from within them. In inner Church matters, the priest sits with leading lay faithful to analyse the challenges facing evangelization in the parish, such as the fall in the percentage of Catholics who come to Sunday Mass, the reasons why many young people are cold towards religious practice, the causes of cohabitation before marriage and what could be done, and the reasons why some sects or new religious movements attract some of our Catholics. The priest will even welcome feed-back from the lay people on the quality of his homilies and on how the people see the *ars celebrandi* as exercised by the priest in their parish. "Ministries and charisms, being diverse and complementary, are all necessary for the Church to grow, each in its own way" (*Christifideles Laici*, 27). "All of us, pastors and lay faithful, have the duty to promote and nourish stronger bonds and mutual esteem, cordiality and collaboration among the various forms of lay associations (*op. cit.*, 31).

For this desirable collaboration to become, and re-main, a reality, it will be required that both clergy and laity should be Christ-centred, not self-centred. They are promoting the Kingdom of Christ, not their individual selves nor their group interests. Priests and lay faithful are not engaging in a power struggle. St Paul's one and only concern was that Christ be preached (cf. Philp 1:15-19). St Paul discouraged those Corinthians who talked of factions for Paul, or for Apollos, or for Cephas or for Christ (cf. I Cor 1:10-16). In constant prayer and humility and in a spirit of readiness to do God's will, the Lord Jesus will make clear to the priest how he should best relate to the lay faithful.

34. The Priest's Relationship with Consecrated Men and Women

The consecrated life is a gift of the Holy Spirit to the Church and to the world. Monks and nuns, religious brothers and sisters and members of secular institutes and other forms of the consecrated life are manifesting that "the Kingdom of God and its overmastering necessities are superior to all earthly considerations" (*Lumen Gentium*, 44). The consecrated life belongs to the life of holiness in the Church. Something would be missing if this state of life were lacking in the Church.

It is expected of the priest that he will take steps to inform himself well on this way of life according as the Church understands it and approves it. The Church documents from *Lumen Gentium* and *Perfectae Caritatis* of the Second Vatican Council, to the many writings of the Popes and the Congregation for Institutes of Consecrated Life and for Societies of Apostolic Life are not lacking. The priest should learn to appreciate what specific charism the Church has approved for the Orders or Congregations of consecrated men and women who are in his parish or with whom he works. If he is going to conduct retreat conferences for them, or to give them a talk or piece of advice, it is helpful that he has read their constitutions.

It seems obvious to say that the priest should respect consecrated men and women and work with them in suitable ways as with co-workers in the vineyard of the Lord. And yet, these relationships sometimes leave much to be desired. It is unpleasant to see a priest who looks down on religious or who assumes that there will be tension in his relations with them. Rather, the priest should regard their charism as God's precious gift to the Church and be a model, also to the lay faithful, on how to work with them for the promotion of the Kingdom of Christ. The priest should also not forget to recommend intentions regarding his parish or other work, to the prayers and sacrifices of monastic communities which may exist in his area.

VII.
THE CROSS IN THE LIFE OF THE PRIEST

35. Suffering and its many origins

Suffering will not be lacking in the life of the priest. It can come in many different forms. Sickness, old age and car accidents bring suffering. Heat, cold, poverty, hunger and an oppressive climate also take their toll. A different type of cross comes from being misunderstood, from false accusation, from contradiction by others and from ingratitude coming from people for whom one has done much.

A subtle type of suffering can arise from people's coldness or hatred towards us (real or imagined), from non-fulfilment of our hopes and from the crashing of our projects. Another priest is pained because he did not get the promotion that he was hoping for, or because he considers that he has again been forgotten by his Superiors. And what shall we say of the priest who suffers because he refuses to accept his limitations whether in intellectual gifts or in physical qualities?

The first approach to be made in facing these situations of suffering is that the priest is to be helped to distinguish between those crosses which Divine Providence has allowed to come his way, and those sufferings which the priest has made for himself. The priest may need a wise spiritual director to help him identify where he himself is the architect of his own misery. If he laments that he was not given a deserved promotion, that he has been forgotten or has been marginalized by his Bishop, that people do not respect him or show him sufficient love, the spiritual director in most of such cases has to advise him to get serious, to get out of his cocoon of self pity, and to stop trying to be a judge in his own case, or imagining situations that have nothing in reality to correspond with them!

Let us therefore talk, not of self-inflicted sufferings, but of crosses like sickness, old age, climate conditions, false accusations and ingratitude which the Lord may allow to come our way.

Jesus Christ is our model. Suffering entered his earthly life from beginning to end, from Bethlehem to Calvary. If God had consulted us, would we have advised that the Son of God made man be born in a stable at Bethlehem because all the rooms in the hotels and hostels had been booked up? Would we not have suggested a small miracle to save the Holy Family the fatigue of the flight into Egypt? Christ was not given a hero's welcome when he preached in the synagogue in Nazareth: would we in the style of the "sons of thunder" James and John have asked Jesus that we be allowed to call down fire from heaven to devour those who were so unfriendly? Christ healed ten lepers and only one remembered to come back and thank him. He fed thousands of people with a few loaves and yet they did not believe that he is the true bread that came down from heaven. The crowd sang "Hosanna to the Son of David" on Palm Sunday and within five days they cried "Crucify him", and there is no record that a group organized themselves to counter this ingratitude. Would our reactions in similar situations have been anything like those of Christ? Jesus went through a mock trial before Pilate and the High Priests where most rules of justice and fairness were violated. The only time Pilate showed courage was when he refused to modify the inscription his administration had pinned to the cross: "What I have written, I have written"!

Indeed Jesus was a man of sorrows and acquainted with suffering (cf. Is 53:3).

Jesus saved us through his suffering and the Cross. If there had been a better road, he would have taught us that. He invites all who want to be his disciples to take up their cross daily and follow him. Does the priest want to be different from his Master? Can he discover a better way to follow Christ? Does he want to arrive at Easter Day without Good Friday? Is it not better and safer for him to leave the unsolved enigma of suffering in the hands of Divine Providence, in the spirit of Psalm 22?

When the priest puts on the vestments and goes to the altar to offer the Eucharistic Sacrifice, he does not go empty-handed. He brings with him his joys and sorrows, projects and plans, disappointments and pains, bitter experiences and ingratitudes received. He offers Christ to God the Father. But he also learns to offer himself through Christ, with Christ and in Christ. In that way, with St Paul, he can "fill up what is lacking in the afflictions of Christ on behalf of his body which is the Church" (Col 1:24). Suffering has salvific value. St Augustine says that God who created us without our cooperation, will not save us without our cooperation (cf. *Sermo* 169,13)

My I repeat the remark that the priest should not increase his suffering by exaggerated imaginations of what people have done to him, or by listening to gossips, or by self-pity. The priest will have enough to suffer in life. There is no need for him to invent a few more crosses!

36. Any use for Trials in Priest's Life?

Suffering in the life of the priest can be looked at as a trial. This is an aspect which deserves further examination. The priest can suffer for objective reasons in the many ways listed in the preceding paragraphs. He can also suffer when he receives punishment under false accusation, or when there is someone whose invitation to the priest to do some evil is rejected by the priest and that spurned person now seeks revenge, like Potiphar's wife against Joseph in Egypt. A priest can also suffer because of the virus of exaggerated tribalism in other people, or simply because someone who is powerful does not like him for no known reason. There have been priests whose suffering comes from some unscrupulous members of their parish council, or from some rich person who felt offended by an objectively innocent and proper homily delivered by the priest.

Trials can serve many purposes. They can be regarded as penance for our sins, and sometimes they are really such, and many even in part be due to our weaknesses. Trials can also be a means to humble our pride so that we realize better our spiritual poverty and fragility, presume less on our own powers and rely more on God. Trials can also serve to purify us, to make our love for God more singleminded. St Francis Xavier prayed thus: "I love you Lord God, not because you can bring me to heaven or send me to hell, but simply because you are who you are: my King and my God". One does not arrive at such a high degree of pure love of God in one day. It is generally the result of long perseverance and the overcoming of many trials.

Trials can help to make us more mature, to lift us to higher levels of freedom, and to manifest of what type is our devotion to God. Job in the Old Testament offers a luminous example of this. The Devil "who accuses our brothers before our God day and night" (Rev 12:10) argues that Job loves God because of self interest. He says that Job's service of God is only a façade, and that if Job is hit in his person, he will abandon all that appearance and curse God. God allowed Satan to try Job. Satan hit him very hard so that his whole body become one putrid sore. But Job remained faithful to God. He passed the test, although he did not know the real reasons for his plight. God rewarded Job in a big way.

On trials which come to us, we should note the following. God does not tempt us to evil (cf James 1:13). But he can allow trials to come to us for the reasons stated above, or for reasons that we do not know. Regarding the man born blind, the Apostles asked Jesus who had sinned: this man or his parents, that he should be born blind? And our Saviour replied: "Neither he nor his parents sinned; it is so that the works of God might be made visible through him" (Jn 9:3). Sometimes when we, or some other people, are under trial, we make judgments on the reasons, and we are wrong. We should not presume that we know all the ways of Divine Providence.

God's Providence can for his own reasons and for his glory send or allow trials on his chosen ones and friends like St Anthony of Egypt, St Teresa d'Avila, St Catherine of Siena, St Padre Pio of Pietrelcina, Blessed Cardinal Ferrari of Milan and Blessed Mother Teresa

VII. The Cross in the Life of the Priest

of Calcutta. If the Eternal Father allowed his Son Incarnate to bear the sufferings due for our sins (cf Is 53:4-7), who are we to think that we know why good people go through trials?

God will never allow us to be tried or tempted beyond what we can bear, "but with the trial he will also provide a way out, so that you may be able to bear it" (I Cor 10:13). We should hope in God and trust in him, and then nothing can separate us from the love of Christ, neither anguish, nor distress, nor persecution, nor famine, nor nakedness, nor peril nor the sword (cf Rm 9:35).

We should, however, note that trials can be dangerous because of the risk of a fall. We should therefore meet trials with prayer and humility. There is no doubt that trials can help us to love God more. And love demands sacrifice, renunciation purification and painful transformation (cf J. Ratzinger/Benedict XVI, *Jesus of Nazareth*, chapter 5, Commentary on *And lead us not into temptation* of the Lord's Prayer, pages 161-164, in English edition by Doubleday).

VIII.
TOWARDS THE
SUNSET OF LIFE

Dear brother priest, you may be young now. But it is clear that, if Go so wills, time will come when you will be on the other side of seventy or eighty years. Let us therefore close this letter with some reflections on the sunset of life.

37. Material Provisions for Older Priests

Every diocese has to ask itself what arrangements it is making to look after the older members of the diocesan presbyterium who are no longer able to carry out the full demands of their priestly ministry. I do not pretend here to be able to give a recipe. But questions like the following may be of help: where are older priests to live? Are they to be looked after in parish rectories where the present pastor is ready and willing to receive them? Is the diocese not wise to think